AZTEC

Mary Stout

Gareth Stevens Publishing

A WORLD ALMANAC EDUCATION GROUP COMPANY

Please visit our web site at: www.garethstevens.com
For a free color catalog describing Gareth Stevens Publishing's list of high-quality books
and multimedia programs, call 1-800-542-2595 (USA) or 1-800-387-3178 (Canada).
Gareth Stevens Publishing's fax: (414) 332-3567.

Library of Congress Cataloging-in-Publication Data

Stout, Mary, 1954-
    Aztec / by Mary Stout.
        p. cm. — (Native American peoples)
    Summary: Describes the origin, history, traditional, and contemporary ways
of life of the Aztec Indians of Mexico.
    Includes bibliographical references and index.
    ISBN 0-8368-3699-5 (lib. bdg.)
    1. Aztecs—Juvenile literature. [1. Aztecs. 2. Indians of Mexico.] I. Title.
II. Series.
F1219.73.S77   2003 2004
972'.00497452—dc21   2003045590

First published in 2004 by
Gareth Stevens Publishing
A World Almanac Education Group Company
330 West Olive Street, Suite 100
Milwaukee, WI 53212 USA

Produced by Discovery Books
Project editor: Valerie J. Weber
Designer and page production: Sabine Beaupré
Photo researcher: Rachel Tisdale
Native American consultant: D. L. Birchfield, J.D., Associate Professor of Native American
  Studies at the University of Lethbridge, Alberta
Maps and diagrams: Stefan Chabluk
Gareth Stevens editorial direction: Mark Sachner
Gareth Stevens art direction: Tammy Gruenewald
Gareth Stevens production: Beth Meinholz and Jessica L. Yanke

Photo credits: Native Stock: cover, pp. 26 (bottom), 27; Werner Forman Archive: pp. 4, 16, 17,
23; Bridgeman Art Library: pp. 5, 26 (top); Peter Newark's American Pictures: pp. 6, 9, 10, 11,
15 (both), 20, 21 (both), 25; Corbis: pp. 8, 14, 18, 19, 22, 24; Courtesy of the Library of
Congress: pp. 12, 13; p. 26 (c) 2003 Banco de Mexico Diego Rivera & Frida Kahlo Museums
Trust. Av. Cinco de Mayo No. 2, Del. Cuauhtemoc 06059, Mexico, D.F.

Printed in the United States of America

1 2 3 4 5 6 7 8 9 07 06 05 04 03

Cover caption: These dancers are dressed in the colorful ceremonial clothes of their
Aztec ancestors.

Contents

Words that appear in the glossary are printed in
boldface type the first time they appear in the text.

Origins

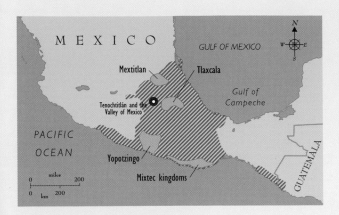

The red markings indicate the areas that the Aztecs conquered. Orange areas are independent territories.

This beautiful mask represents one of the most powerful creator gods, Tezcatlipoca. He was called the "Smoking Mirror."

Land of the Aztecs

The Aztecs were an early Native American tribe who lived in central Mexico from about 1325 to 1519, when Spanish **conquistadors** destroyed them. Although the Aztecs don't exist as a tribe today, their **descendants** and those of other Nahuatl-speaking tribes from that time are known today as the Nahuas and number about 1.4 million.

Aztec Creation Story

Like many ancient cultures, the Aztecs told an origin story that explained the history of the world. They believed that the earth was previously created and destroyed four times.

Quetzalcoatl and Tezcatlipoca, creators of the fifth world, found the earth covered with water, with only a giant monster living there. The gods tore the monster in two: the upper part of his body became land, and the lower part was thrown into the sky to become the stars. Two other gods, Nanaautzin and Tecuciztecatl, threw themselves into fire to become the Sun and Moon. Quetzalcoatl then created humans by going to the underworld of the dead and gathering some old bones that he ground up and sprinkled with his own blood.

No one knows for sure how the Aztecs and other Indians came to North America. Some scientists say that they may have come from people who crossed a landmass across the Bering Strait from Siberia to Alaska and walked down to Central America a long time ago. Others think people came from Asia by boat and landed in the Americas.

This page from an Aztec book, shows the Aztecs leaving Aztlan to journey to their new home.

The Wanderers

The wandering Aztecs called themselves *Mexica* and began their journey at a place known as Aztlan. Because of the Mexicas' origins, other people called them "Aztecs." Leaving Aztlan as instructed by their god Huitzilopochtli, the Aztecs traveled for many years, looking for their new home, which they would recognize by a sign — an eagle perched on a cactus with a snake in its beak.

The Nahuatl Language

The Nahuatl language was spoken by the Aztecs and is still spoken today in the country of Mexico.

Nahuatl	Pronunciation	English
amatl	a-matl	codex
atl	a-tl	water
calli	kal-li	house
chocolatl	cho-ko-latl	chocolate
pilli	pil-li	noble person
pochtecatl	poch-te-katl	merchant
telpochcalli	tel-poch-kal-li	school, college
teocalli	te-o-kal-li	temple

Chapter 2

History

The first page of the *Codex Mendoza*, a book written by an unknown Aztec artist for the first Spanish governor of New Spain, tells the story of the Aztecs settling in Tenochtitlán. It is also a map of this island city-state.

The Rise of the Aztecs

In 1168, the Aztecs came to the Valley of Mexico, which was already home to many other people. These people were descendants of the Toltecs, an advanced warrior society that ruled Mexico from the tenth to the twelfth centuries. The Aztecs claimed descent from the Chichimecs, a wild, wandering, and warlike people.

Eventually, the Aztecs settled near the Culhuas, who ruled them. The warlike Aztecs became hired soldiers who helped the Culhuas defeat neighboring tribes in battle. A grateful Culhua chief gave his daughter to the Aztec chief to marry, but instead she was **sacrificed** to their god Huitzilopochtli, which angered the Culhuas. War broke out between the Culhuas and the Aztecs, and the Aztecs fled to a swampy island in the middle of Lake Texcoco. Here, the Aztecs saw an eagle perched on a cactus with a snake in its mouth, just as their god had predicted. They immediately began building their new home on the island, a city named Tenochtitlán, in 1325.

Tenochtitlán was on an island in the middle of Lake Texcoco, reached only by four causeways (raised roads through water). Canals (shown in blue) crisscross the island. The Axayacatl Palace, originally where an earlier Aztec ruler lived, became the guest house for the Spanish army when Emperor Motecuhzoma (also spelled *Montezuma*) first welcomed them to Tenochtitlán.

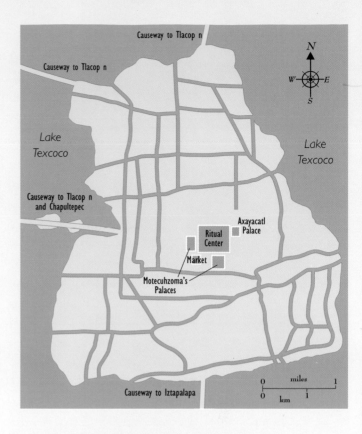

The Aztec Empire

The Aztecs became stronger and more powerful on their island city, and their warriors began to conquer neighboring tribes. During the mid-1400s, an agreement with two other **city-states** created the ruling Triple **Alliance**, made up of Tenochtitlán, Texcoco, and Tlacopán. These three city-states ruled over 12 million people in the Valley of Mexico. Though required

Chinampas

The chinampas, or "floating gardens," were the Aztecs' clever solution to the problem of how to expand a city that was on an island in the middle of a lake. First, they wove reeds together to form a raftlike base. Then they brought soil by canoe from the mainland to put on the reeds. Built in shallow water near shore, chinampas were held in place by posts sunk into the lakebed and by the roots of trees and plants. The Aztecs planted food crops and built thatched houses on the chinampas.

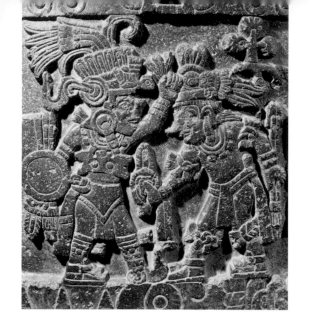

An Aztec sculpture. Aztec warriors were skillful and fierce — but they didn't try to kill their enemies. Their main job was to capture prisoners and conquer new lands so their people would pay tribute to the Aztecs.

Paying Tribute to the Aztecs

One Aztec book, the *Codex Mendoza*, records the tribute sent to the Aztecs by various people. The twice-yearly tribute of the province of Xoconosco consisted of:

2 jade necklaces

2,400 bundles of colored feathers

160 pelts of blue cotinga (birds)

800 bundles of yellow feathers

800 bundles of long quetzal bird tail feathers

2 lip plugs made of amber and gold

200 loads of cocoa beans

40 jaguar skins

800 gourd bowls

2 bricks of amber

to pay **tribute** to the Triple Alliance, the conquered people were left alone. They had to send bird feathers (highly valued for majestic cloaks and head-dresses), food, jewelry, cocoa beans, slaves, and other valuables to Tenochtitlán twice a year. Many of the conquered people were unhappy with their rulers since they had to pay such huge tributes.

The Spanish Conquest

In 1519, Hernán Cortés, a Spanish conquistador, arrived in Mexico. He was searching for gold, but he also wanted to win lands for the Spanish kingdom and souls for his Catholic religion. Motecuhzoma II (also spelled *Montezuma*), the Aztec emperor, knew of Cortés's arrival from his spies. Though Motecuhzoma refused his requests to visit the capital city, Cortés decided to march to Tenochtitlán anyway. On his way, he passed through the lands of the Totonacs, who joined the Spanish conquistadors and encouraged Cortés to defeat the Aztecs.

La Malinche

A young Native woman helped Hernán Cortés conquer Tenochtitlán. Malintzin (also called Dona Marina or La Malinche) was one of the slaves given to Cortés after he defeated a coastal tribe. Only fourteen years old, she spoke both Maya and Nahuatl and quickly learned Spanish. With Malintzin at his side translating, Cortés could communicate with the people of the Aztec Empire. She helped Cortés convince other tribes to join the Spanish to defeat the Aztecs. While many Native Americans respected her power, others disliked her for helping the Spanish to take over Mexico. Today, Mexicans still use "La Malinche" to refer to a traitor.

Cortés and his army of five hundred men came to Mexico by ship from Cuba, another Spanish colony. Cortés's men were afraid of the Natives and wanted to return, so Cortés burned his own boats. His men had no choice but to follow him as he marched on and destroyed Tenochtitlán.

Guests Take a Prisoner

Since he had no choice, Motecuhzoma at last invited Cortés to come to Tenochtitlán, treating the Spaniards as honored guests. In return, however, Cortés took the emperor prisoner. Motecuhzoma's brother, Cuitlahuac, led the Aztec warriors against the Spanish conquistadors and drove them out of Tenochtitlán in a fierce battle that ended with two-thirds of the conquistadors dead. During the battle, Motecuhzoma was also killed. While Cortés planned a new attack on Tenochtitlán, Cuitlahuac became the new emperor.

And the fighting men were all very well armed and bedecked with feathers, white, red, yellow, blue, green, black, and every colour, all with different plumes on their heads and backs; round their necks they wore many jewels of gold, set with stones, as well as bracelets of brilliant gold . . .

Spanish priest Fray Duran describing Aztec noble warriors setting out to conquer another tribe

The Spanish conquest of Mexico as portrayed in an Aztec book of pictures. The Native Americans were amazed and frightened by the ships, horses, and guns owned by the Spanish.

Motecuhzoma II

Motecuhzoma II became the Aztec emperor in 1502, when he was about thirty-three years old. Although he was a respected warrior, he showed uncertainty in dealing with Cortés and the Spaniards. Cortés told Motecuhzoma he was a friendly ambassador from Spain, and the king of Texcoco advised him to treat the Spaniards as friends. However, Motecuhzoma's brother and his cousin thought that Cortés was an enemy invader who should be attacked. Other advisors suggested that Cortés might be a returning god.

After Cortés imprisoned him in his own palace, Motecuhzoma stood on his roof and asked his people to stop fighting when they rose up against the Spanish invaders. They ignored him, and Motecuhzoma was killed in the battle that took place. No one knows for sure whether he was killed by the Spanish or the Aztecs.

Although the Spaniards did not plan on it, they brought another threat to the Aztecs in the form of a deadly disease — **smallpox** — to which the Natives had no **immunity**. A smallpox **epidemic** broke out, killing many Aztecs, including the new emperor. In 1521, a young man called Cuauhtemoc, the last Aztec emperor, prepared for Cortés's attack. After seventy-five days of fierce battles in the city, the Spanish triumphed and the Aztecs surrendered.

After the Conquest

After the Aztecs surrendered to the Spanish, their Native American enemies continued to kill the Aztecs and destroy Tenochtitlán. One source listed the death toll at 117,000 people. The city lay in ruins; many survivors left to settle elsewhere. Putting Emperor Cuauhtemoc in prison, the conquistadors made slaves of the surviving Aztec warriors.

An Aztec illustration shows the Spanish killing Motecuhzoma and dumping his body into a Tenochtitlán canal. The Spanish books say that the Aztecs killed their own emperor by throwing stones at him. Motecuhzoma's death remains a mystery to this day.

After the Spanish conquered the Aztecs, the Native people still paid tribute — this time to the Spanish instead of Motecuhzoma. This record of the tribute paid in 1531 is written in the same manner that the Aztecs always kept their records.

Let me tell you about the dead bodies. I swear that all the houses on the lake were full of heads and corpses. . . . The streets, squares, houses, and courts were filled with bodies so that it was almost impossible to pass. Even Cortés was sick.

Bernal Diaz del Castillo, a Spaniard who traveled with Cortés, writing about Tenochtitlán after the Aztec defeat

To reward his men, Cortés set up a system of *encomiendas,* giving them large areas of land and the Native slaves to work it. He rebuilt the city of Tenochtitlán, calling it Mexico City after the Mexican people, which is still its name today. Other changes followed: settlers were encouraged to come from Spain, Aztec schools were closed, and Christian schools were opened.

Diseases brought by the Spanish continued to kill the Native American people. Although 25 million Native American people lived in Mexico when the Spanish arrived, by 1592, the population had dropped to less than 2 million.

A Mix of Cultures

Mexico City became the capital of a Spanish colony called New Spain, and boatloads of Spanish people continued to come and settle in the new land, growing sugarcane and mining silver. The Natives became a part of the lower **class** of the **colonial** society, working for the Spanish. The Spanish brought the Catholic religion, and many Natives became Catholic and were educated in Christian schools. The two cultures began to blend together, a process that continued for over two hundred years.

When Mexico became independent of Spain in 1821, the people began to look at their Aztec heritage with pride. Their heritage showed in the new Mexican national flag, which represented the Aztec story — an eagle perched on a cactus with a snake in its mouth. The descendants of all of the different Native American tribes living in the Valley of Mexico became known as Nahuas since they all spoke Nahuatl. By the 1910 Mexican Revolution, most Nahuas also had Spanish ancestors, because of many marriages between Spanish and Natives in the past. Today, Mexican culture is a mixture of Spanish, Aztec, and other Native heritages.

Thousands of Aztecs died from the smallpox disease itself and more died from hunger. So many people were ill that there was no one left to care for them. Today, people wonder if the Aztecs might have defeated the Spanish had they not been so sick with smallpox.

Traditional Way of Life

In Aztec society, clothing was based on social class. Only nobles wore clothes made of cotton with bright colors, rich decorations, and feathers.

Aztec Society

Aztec society was highly organized, and each person knew his or her place in it from birth. At the top were the nobles, who owned the land, ran the government, and were in charge of the army. Because they spoke with the gods and acted as leaders, priests were also important in Aztec society. The Aztec middle class was made up of merchants and highly skilled artisans, such as the feather workers and stonemasons. The commoners, or lower class, were farmers, soldiers, and laborers.

The lowest class were slaves. While some slaves were captured in war, sometimes Aztecs sold themselves into slavery if they couldn't make a living. If a commoner didn't pay his taxes, he could become a slave. If he became a successful soldier or priest, however, he could become one of the lower class of nobles; all of the highest nobles were born into their class.

All of the people, except for the nobles, were expected to pay a tax or contribute labor to the nobles.

This life-size carving of an Aztec eagle warrior shows him wearing the feathered helmet shaped like an eagle's head with its mouth open.

Aztec Warriors

The Aztecs battled neighboring Natives to take captives, who were then offered for sacrifice at the top of the temple steps in Tenochtitlán. Although human sacrifice to the gods existed in other cultures, the thirsty Aztec gods required much more blood than others.

Important people in Aztec society, warriors could be from the noble or lower classes. As in today's military, their dress reflected their rank. A warrior who took one captive in war without help carried an oak club and a plain shield and wore a cloak decorated with flowers. A two-captive warrior could wear sandals, a cone-shaped hat, and a feathered suit. The four-captive warrior was allowed to wear an outfit made with jaguar skin. Known as "eagle warriors," the top warriors wore eagle feathers and helmets shaped like eagle heads.

The artisans gave the nobles feather cloaks, **obsidian** blades, ceramic figures, or other products of their work. Farmers contributed food and labor; for example, their wives might weave for the nobles for several weeks each year.

First a Thief, Then a Slave

The organized Aztecs also had a legal system with many judges and courts. Nobles and commoners went to different courts. Aztec records show more than eighty crimes listed with punishments. The most serious crimes were theft, murder, and public drunkenness. As a punishment for stealing, a thief was made a slave to the person from whom he or she stole.

Childhood and Marriage

Children were important to all Aztecs, nobles and commoners alike. Four days after birth, a **midwife** took the Aztec child outside for a ritual bath, and symbols of the baby's life were placed in its hands. For example, a boy baby might be given a little shield and arrow.

When children were three years old, they began to be taught by their parents how to help and were given small tasks. Sometime between the ages of seven and fourteen, the children were sent to school. All Aztec children attended school, but there were different schools for nobles and commoners.

Sculpture of a girl. When an Aztec baby girl was given her first ritual bath, symbols of her future life, such as a little red basket and a weaver's tools, were placed in her hands.

16

Girls were ready for marriage at age fifteen or later, and boys were usually ready when they finished school at age twenty. Following the selection of a lucky wedding day according to the Aztec calendar, a large celebration and feast were prepared. At the end of the first day, the bride and groom sat on a mat in front of a fire. Their **matchmaker** tied the ends of the bride's and groom's new capes together, and they were married. Often, the wedding party continued for a week.

Class Affects Housing and Clothing

Aztec homes were different depending upon the class of the owner. Nobles lived in large two-story homes with many rooms, made with stone walls and log-and-plaster roofs, while commoners lived in huts made from **adobe** bricks with thatched roofs.

The clothing worn by the Aztecs was also based on their social class. Only nobles wore capes made of beautiful bird feathers and jewelry of gold and turquoise or jade stones. Excellent weavers,

Most Aztec households used bowls and drinking cups made from clay. These beautifully designed cups were used by a noble household. Noble homes also held clay figurines and decorations.

Aztec Games: Better Not Lose . . .

The Aztecs enjoyed games, including *patolli*, a board game like backgammon, and a ball game called *tlachtli*, which was also played by the Mayans and other Central American peoples. Two teams of two or three people played tlachtli on a court shaped like a capital "I." Stone rings were attached 27 feet (8 meters) high on each side of the court. Players put on padded knee, arm, and hip protectors and tried to knock the hard rubber ball through the rings, mostly with their hips. This game also had religious connections, as the ball represented the Sun and Moon, and the ball court was the world. The Aztecs believed that the outcome of a ball game could sometimes foretell the future, and nobles would often bet on the game. At times, the losing team would be sacrificed.

Shaped like the head of a macaw bird, this ball-game marker is from one of the ancient tlachtli ball courts. Although we know stone markers were placed on the ground in the ball courts, no one is sure how they were used during the game.

Aztec women used the fibers from cotton, maguey (agave), and hemp plants to make into cloth. Women usually wore skirts and *huipiles* (a type of blouse), and men wore loincloths and capes.

Aztecs grew a variety of food crops, including corn, beans, onions, peppers, tomatoes, squash, and fruit. They also ate fish, ducks, and turkeys. Only nobles were allowed to hunt larger animals. One favorite Aztec food was **tamales**, which the bride and groom ate as part of their wedding ceremony.

The Arts

The Aztecs believed that art was a reflection of and communication with the gods. Their culture was richly artistic, and the style of their art was rooted in the Toltec culture. The Aztecs deeply appreciated speeches and poetry, some of which survive, like this poem about Tenochtitlán:

The city is spread out in circles of jade,
Radiating flashes of light like quetzal plumes.
Beside it lords are borne in boats:
Over them extends a flowery mist.

Their sculptors carved calendars, gods, goddesses, and animals from stone and created beautiful mosaics from precious stones. Jewelers made intricate jewelry from gold and precious stones. However, the most valued art form was feather work. Skilled artisans created amazing headdresses and capes from the brightly colored feathers of tropical birds, such as the quetzal, parrot, macaw, and hummingbird, for the nobles to wear.

The Aztecs actually had two calendar systems to keep track of days. Weighing 25 tons (23 metric tons) and measuring 12 feet (3.6 m) in diameter, this stone shows the symbols for the Aztec months but does not actually function as a working calendar. The sun god is in the center of the stone, which shows the four previous worlds.

Codices: Aztec Picture Books

The Aztecs used a picture-based writing system to create painted books called **codices** (singular: codex). They folded deerskin or paper made from bark to form books. Then, painters made dyes from ashes and plants and painted their stories on the codices. For example, a picture of a shield and arrows meant war, and one of footprints told of a journey. The painted symbol for Tenochtitlán was a picture of a cactus on a rock. Not only were Aztec codices full of information, but they were beautiful works of art as well.

After the conquest, the Spanish tried to destroy all of the codices and replace them with their own writing system and their own books. Fifteen codices still exist today, however; we can read them to find out about the Aztecs from their own writings.

This picture from the *Florentine Codex* shows Aztec goldsmiths at work.

Quetzalcoatl, whose name means "Feathered Serpent," was one of the most important gods of ancient Mexico. Originally worshiped by the Toltecs, Quetzalcoatl was also honored by the Aztecs as a one of the creators of the world.

Religious Beliefs

The Aztecs had too many gods to count: one source says over sixteen hundred. As the Aztecs expanded their empire and conquered other tribes, they also included the conquered tribes' gods with their own. Some gods were considered more important than others, however; in fact, the Great Pyramid of Tenochtitlán, in the center of the city, contains only two temples. One is the sacred space for Huitzilopochtli, the Aztecs' ancestor god of the Sun, war, and sacrifice. The other is for Tlaloc, the god of rain. While war was important in Aztec society, rain was crucial for crops to grow.

The chief god of the fifth world in which the Aztecs lived was Tonatiuh, the old Sun god. Quetzalcoatl, a special helper to the Aztec priests, was a god of creation and the wind. The Aztecs believed that someday, earthquakes would destroy this world and that sky monsters would eat the people.

Connected with fate, both good and bad, Tezcatlipoca was important to Aztec rulers, who often prayed to this god known as "Night Wind."

Human Sacrifice

The Aztecs believed that it was the task of humans to sacrifice themselves to keep the Sun moving and the world going. The Sun god fought a daily battle in the sky; human blood was a necessary food for the Sun to continue rising.

Sacrifices were only carried out as religious rituals by priests in temples. The type of sacrifice depended upon which god was being

An Aztec priest, wearing a white cape, performs a ritual human sacrifice to honor and feed the gods.

honored. Humans sacrificed to the rain god were drowned; victims of other sacrifices might be shot with arrows or dropped from a high place. To honor Huitzilopochtli, the hearts of enemy captives were cut out with sharp obsidian blade knives and offered, still beating, to the Sun. The Aztecs honored the victims of the sacrifices, usually enemy warriors, and treated them like gods before their sacrifice. They were assured of a place in heaven.

Gods and Souls

According to the Aztec creation story, when this world was created, two gods volunteered to sacrifice themselves to become the Sun and Moon. Once created, however, the Sun didn't move in the sky until two more gods were sacrificed. Quetzalcoatl, creator of the fifth world, cut open their chests and offered their hearts to Tonatiuh, the Sun god.

The Aztecs believed that each person had three souls. The cause of a person's death determined how long their three souls would travel. The souls of people who died ordinary deaths took a four-year journey to the underworld, and they were buried or cremated with tools and weapons to help them on their travels. People who were sacrificed or killed in war went to various places in the heavens, and their souls only took eighty days to reach their destination.

Another Aztec god, Xipe Totoc ("Our Flayed Lord") was an agricultural god of seeds and fertility. Here, he is shown wearing the skin of a human sacrifice to represent seeds bursting from their skins to grow.

23

Today

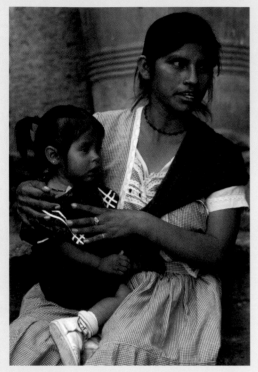

This Nahua woman and her daughter are descendants of the ancient Nahuatl-speaking tribes in Mexico. Today, more than one million Nahuas still speak Nahuatl, the language of the ancient Aztecs.

The Nahua Today

The modern Nahuas are Indians who are descended from one of the Nahuatl-speaking tribes that lived in the Valley of Mexico during the 1500s, including the Aztecs of Tenochtitlán, as well as Natives from other city-states. Over the years, marriage between the Spaniards and Nahuas has resulted in a new Mexican culture that has borrowed elements from both cultures. The most important surviving element of Nahua culture is the Nahuatl language, which is still spoken today.

The Aztec Culture continues

Most Indians became Christians after the Spanish conquest, worshiping in churches built on the same spot where Aztec temples had been torn down. The Natives no longer practiced human sacrifice, their government was destroyed, and their trade and tribute **economy** was replaced. However, Indian peasant communities continued to build adobe houses and make and use household goods and tools much as the Aztecs did. Their foods — corn, beans, tomatoes, chilies, and squashes — are the same as Aztec foods. In some villages today, women continue to spin thread by hand and weave it on a back-strap loom that is similar to the looms used by the Aztec women.

The problems that Nahuas face today are the same as those experienced by many Indians. They are poor and live in rural areas without enough hospitals or schools. They don't have good jobs unless they move to the cities, and there isn't much for young people to do.

The Virgin of Guadalupe

When the Spanish first introduced the god of their Christian religion, the Aztecs welcomed the new Christian god and saints as they had the gods of all their enemies. Over the years, the Nahuas connected some Christian saints with the Aztec traditional gods.

In Mexico today, the Virgin of Guadalupe is a very important religious figure. She is a brown-skinned Mother of God who appeared in 1531 to Juan Diego, a poor Nahua man, and spoke to him in Nahuatl, saying she would protect Native people. This event happened in a place sacred to the Aztec mother goddess Tonantzin, and many experts think that the Virgin of Guadalupe is a blend of the Virgin Mary and Tonantzin.

The Virgin of Guadalupe remains an important religious figure for Mexicans. On December 12 each year, millions gather in churches all over the country to pray, celebrate, and honor *La Reina de México* (the Queen of Mexico).

Proud of his country's Aztec heritage, Mexican artist Diego Rivera often featured Mexico's early history in his murals. This 1950 mural, *The Culture of Totonaken,* shows the nobles of the Totonac city-state visiting the market in Tenochtitlán to trade with the Aztecs.

Contemporary Aztec Influence

Although the Aztec civilization no longer exists as it did in the 1500s, modern Mexican culture reflects its Aztec heritage and spirit. The main language of Mexico, Spanish, uses many Aztec words such as *tomate, chocolat,* and *tamale.* Aztec temples are now museums and contain Aztec art.

Markets featuring colorful arts and crafts of Aztec design can be found in many places in Mexico today.

The careful preservation and study of their Aztec history reflects the pride Mexicans have in their heritage. Twentieth-century Mexican artists such as Diego Rivera created colorful murals containing Aztec symbols, faces, and scenes. Large Mexican marketplaces still sell traditional Aztec crafts such as woven cloth, carved wood, and pottery. Aztec influence is strongly felt in dances and celebrations.

Modern-day descendants of the Aztecs, members of the Efigenio family dress in traditional clothing of the noble class.

Today, one can even see the *volador,* an Aztec dance in which men dressed as colorful birds are attached by ropes to a tall pole and descend it by swinging around and around. The Aztecs continue to live on in many aspects of current Mexican culture.

Day of the Dead

One of the most important Mexican celebrations today is called *Dia de los Muertos,* or Day of the Dead. During the celebration, which usually occurs during a week at the end of October and beginning of November, ancestors are honored in ceremonies that have many Aztec elements. Mexicans create an altar honoring the dead family member(s) and place food and **incense** on it as an offering, just as the Aztecs did. The decorations on the altars often include skulls — a popular Aztec image — made of sugar. It is believed that the spirits of the dead return to the earth to connect with their living family members for a short period of time, then return to the grave.

Time Line

1168   Aztecs wander into the Valley of Mexico.

1325   Aztecs flee to an island and begin building Tenochtitlán.

1427   The Triple Alliance is formed between three city-states: Tenochtitlán, Texcoco, and Tlacopán.

1440   Motecuhzoma I begins his rule as emperor of the Aztecs; Aztec civilization is at its peak.

1502   Motecuhzoma II becomes emperor of the Aztecs.

1519   The population of Mexico is 25 million Native people; Hernán Cortés arrives in Mexico.

1520   Aztecs defeat Cortés, who is forced to retreat.

1521   The Aztecs surrender to the Spanish conquistadors; Tenochtitlán is destroyed and Mexico City is built on the same site.

1525   Cortés named governor-general of New Spain (Mexico).

1531   The Virgin of Guadalupe appears to Juan Diego.

1592   The Native population of Mexico drops to less than 2 million people.

1821   Mexico gains independence from Spain; renewal of interest in Aztec heritage.

Glossary

adobe: a building material made of mud mixed with straw.

alliance: an agreement among two or more groups to work together on a common goal.

city-states: large cities and the area surrounding each that are independent and have their own rulers.

class: divisions of society into social groups that are alike in some way. A society is often divided into upper, middle, and lower classes.

codices: handwritten books made of picture symbols painted on paper. The singular of *codices* is *codex*.

colonial: relating to a colony, an area controlled by another nation.

conquistadors: Spanish conquerors.

descendants: all of the children and children's children of an individual or group; those who come after.

economy: the way a country or people produces, divides up, and uses its goods and money.

epidemic: a sudden increase of a rapidly spreading disease.

immunity: natural protection from a disease.

incense: a substance that has a pleasant smell when burned.

matchmaker: a person who arranges a marriage between two people.

midwife: a woman who helps other women give birth to their babies.

obsidian: a dark, natural glass formed by cooling lava.

sacrifice: to offer something to the gods as an act of worship; often involves killing an animal or a person.

smallpox: a disease that causes a high fever and small bumps and that is passed on easily from person to person.

tamales: ground meat rolled in cornmeal dough, then wrapped in corn husks and steamed.

tribute: a payment by one ruler or nation to another to show that it has been conquered.

More Resources

Web Sites:

http://www.eduscapes.com/42explore/aztec.htm An educational web site about the Aztecs with activities and good links.

http://www.pbs.org/wnet/nature/spirits/html/body_aztec.html A PBS website about the Aztecs that includes a map.

http://www.wsu.edu/~dee/CIVAMRCA/AZTECS.HTM A description of the Aztec civilization with pictures.

http://archaeology.asu.edu/tm/index2.htm A web site about Tenochtitlán's main temple, which is now a museum in Mexico City.

Videos:

The Aztec Empire. The History Channel, 1997.

The Aztecs. Films for the Humanities and Sciences, 1999.

The Aztecs: People of the Sun. Babbitt Instructional Resources, 1998.

The Five Suns: A Sacred History of Mexico. University of California Extension Center for Media and Independent Learning, 1996.

Books:

Baquedano, Elizabeth. *Aztec, Inca & Maya.* Dorling Kindersley, 2000.

Barghusen, Joan D. *The Aztecs: End of a Civilization.* Lucent Books, 2000.

Chrisp, Peter. *The Aztecs* (History Beneath Your Feet). Steck-Vaughn, 2000.

Dawson, Imogen. *Clothes and Crafts in Aztec Times* (Clothes and Crafts in History). Gareth Stevens Publishing, 2000.

Hull, Robert. *The Aztecs* (The Ancient World). Steck-Vaughn, 1998.

Macdonald, Fiona. *Step into the . . . Aztec & Maya Worlds* (Step Into). Lorenz Books, 1998.

Rees, Rosemary. *The Aztecs* (Understanding People in the Past). Heineman Library, 1999.

Thomson, Ruth. *Aztecs: Facts, Things to Make, Activities* (Craft Topics). Franklin Watts, 1999.

Things to Think About and Do

Every Picture Tells a Story

Make a codex. Fold a large sheet of white paper into a screen or fan. Each fold will be a page of your codex. Now draw a story on your codex, using picture symbols — no words — to tell your story. You may make up your own picture symbols to use.

Mexican Flag

Draw a picture of the flag of Mexico. Write down the meaning of the Aztec symbols on the flag.

Invaders! What to Do?

Each group of four to six people should pretend that they are Motecuhzoma II and his advisors. Some strangers have been seen entering your area. You know nothing about them. What should you do about it? Remember, you are the most powerful and feared people in Central America. Report back on your discussion and decisions.

You Are There

Imagine that you are an Aztec boy or girl. Where do you think you would fit in Aztec society? What do you think your life would be like? How is it the same or different from what it is now? What do your parents do in Aztec society? What will you do when you grow up in Tenochtitlán? Explain your thoughts in a brief essay.

Index